Offline Shopping Hacks

Offline Shopping Hacks

15 Simple Practical Hacks to Save Money Shopping Offline

Life 'n' Hack

ISBN 978-1-544-60934-8

Printed in the United States of America

First Edition

KEYS

INFO INTRO: Irreplaceable Real-Time Shopping

- 9 -

HACK #1: Utilize Shopping Search Engines First and Foremost

- 13 -

HACK #2: Subscribe and Request Coupons

- 16 -

HACK #3: Register for Store's Loyalty Points Program

- 18 -

HACK #4: Visit Coupon Aggregators

- 20 -

HACK #5: Map Out Shopping Route

- 23 -

HACK #6: Prioritize with Shopping Pyramid

- 26 -

HACK #7: The Envelope Technique

- 29 -

HACK #8: Operation Shopping Squad

- 32 -

HACK #9: Target Specialty Stores

- 36 -

HACK #10: Bulk Up at Warehouses

- 38 -

HACK #11: Pierce into YOUR Shopping Crystal Ball

- 41 -

HACK #12: Two Time's a Charm for Any Out-of-Season
Items

- 44 -

HACK #13: Luxury for Less

- 46 -

HACK #14: Shopping Locally at the Perishables' Source

- 49 -

HACK #15: Stretching the Dollar for Brand Names

- 53 -

INFO UNLOCKED: Going Pro in Offline Shopping

- 56 -

Offline Shopping Hacks

INFO INTRO:

Irreplaceable Real-Time Shopping

It may be hard to imagine, but in the not too distant past the only way to shop was to physically set foot in a store. But with the advent of the internet, online shopping exploded in popularity as a more convenient option to traditional shopping.

And for good reason! It's quite easy to see the advantages of online shopping. It can be done at any time and from anywhere with an internet connection. When compared with loud, busy shopping malls, who wouldn't prefer to shop in their pajamas from the comfort of their couch?

Online shopping also makes hard-to-find products like rare CD's, collectibles, or electronics just a few clicks away. It's as if the whole world is literally at your fingertips.

However, don't be too hasty and write off in-store shopping altogether! Offline shopping has its own benefits worth considering. Traditional in-store shopping provides shoppers with the irreplaceable ability to touch or test the product and evaluate it in person before deciding to purchase.

For example, if you were buying an Italian fruitcake for Christmas you wouldn't dare order it online. Instead, you would go to your nearest grocery store or bakery to check the quality of cakes they sell. You would be able to determine they are fresh by checking the expiration date and the country of provenance (to verify if it's really an Italian product). Basically, who buys perishable goods (like milk or any delicate food) online? The same goes for that expensive pair of jeans you've been looking to buy.

This way you are likely to get the best possible product, which is not always the case when you order something online having it turned out different from what you expected.

Offline, in-store shopping offers the following advantages:

- **Quality control**: You get to touch, taste or inspect the product in-person to more accurately determine quality.

- **Evaluate value**: You can judge which product is worth buying by comparing the price to the actual value of the product.

- **Social experience**: Shopping in-store facilitates interactions with the store's staff to gain advice and guidance. You will also have the opportunity to speak with other customers who may know a valuable secret or two about a specific product.

- **Exposure to new products**: While in store, you are bound to discover new or related products to enhance your experience. It's very possible to leave the store with more than expected (better deals, better options, etc.).

All this sounds wonderful, right?

While offline shopping can be relaxing—even therapeutic at times—it can also get overwhelming, not to mention a toll on your wallet/purse if you are not doing it properly. So, we've compiled a list of some the best shopping strategies you need to know before heading out the door.

Read on to learn how you can start shopping offline efficiently, effectively, and economically.

HACK #1:

Utilize Shopping Search Engines First and Foremost

Knowing equals saving, especially when it comes to shopping. If you want the best product at the best price, then do your homework! The internet makes it easy to research products and get the information like price, dimensions, and shipping costs, just to name a few.

Popular sites that are especially helpful in this process are shopping search engines like Pricegrabber.com, Nextag.com, or Google shopping. Take advantage of these sites by making note of the following:

- **Price range:** Collect prices from several sites to help you set a budget.

- **Manufacturer**: Noting the manufacturer is an important factor when judging the quality of a product. Certain brands have better reputations than others. Of course, once you are at the store, you'll be able to assess the quality in person.

- **Options**: Style, color and measurement options are also important, because they help you choose the item that meets your needs best. Once at the store, you will save time by knowing exactly what you need.

- **Product alternatives**: These sites can also help you pick a second option, in case your chosen model, color or size is out of stock. This way you still get to shop effectively and come out of the store satisfied.

Make sure you keep these details handy to compare with the products you find in store. For convenience, you can even take a snapshot of the screen to verify the information you found online.

<u>ASSIGNMENT</u>: Now, try it out for yourself! Visit Pricegrabber.com, Nextag.com, and Google shopping to familiarize yourself with choosing and comparing products. Make sure to include prices, sizes, and other characteristics to narrow down the choices.

HACK #2:

Subscribe and Request Coupons

Would you believe that all you need to do to score major discounts on your favorite products is to ask? That's right! Most companies are more than happy to send you coupons in the mail if you ask to be added to the store's mailing list.

Below is a list of a few ideas to get you started. You will be amazed by how easy and worthwhile it is:

- Sign up with a family brand, like Kellogg's family reward. This company sends coupons every month that you can print off and use in stores.

- Email your favorite companies. Their email is usually provided on the company's website. All you have to do is tell them how much you like their products, and they will offer to add you to their mailing list.

- You can also go to the Facebook page of your favorite companies and 'Like' them. The company will then post promotional offers that will show up in your Facebook Newsfeed. This is also a great way to keep up-to-date on any new product offerings.

Getting free coupons is easier than you think and can pay off big time! Use them to score killer deals when shopping offline.

ASSIGNMENT: Your assignment is to explore these various options for yourself and start raking in the savings.

HACK #3:

Register for Store's Loyalty Points Program

There are websites specifically designed to save you big money in the checkout lines of your favorite stores. Hard to believe, huh? Sites like Plenti.com allow you to earn points on products that you buy all the time. That means that you earn points each and every time you checkout!

Here's how to get started:

1. Go to Plenti.com and see if any of the stores you shop is listed on there, then register online with your name and email address.

2. Earn points when shopping with the site's partners—usually restaurants, insurance companies, pharmacies, major retail stores, travel agencies, satellite TV providers, etc.

3. Use your accumulated points when you check out to score amazing discounts.

See how easy it is?

ASSIGNMENT: Now it's your turn to try. Register for a loyalty program/point program and start earning points. You will love watching them rack up every time you shop.

HACK #4:

Visit Coupon Aggregators

Coupon aggregator websites alert you to available coupons and even tries them automatically! The whole process takes a few seconds and provides you with the best manufacturer coupons, promotional code coupons or free coupon codes.

The most popular coupon aggregator sites you should check out are RetailMeNot.com, Coupons.com, Groupons.com, MoneySavingMom.com, TheKrazyCouponLady.com, Yipit.com, Amazon Gold Box Deals, Woot.com, Slickdeals.net, Fatwallet.com, Reddit.com and Joinpiggy.com

Before you get started, you need to know the following:

- Most aggregator sites don't require you to sign up or open an account with them.

- All you have to do is type in your store, pick the coupon you need and print it out.

- Most of these sites provide you with coupons in various categories like food, home, computers, kids, etc. Some sites, like RetailMeNot.com, even allow you to provide feedback that can be of use to other shoppers.

Now that you know how simple it is to use coupon aggregators, why don't you give it a whirl?

ASSIGNMENT: Peruse several of the sites mentioned above and check out the available deals. Pick coupons that you are sure you can use. Then evaluate each site, and rate their pros and cons. For example, which ones provide the most useful coupons? Which sites seem to have coupons with high rejection rates? This way, you can eliminate the less effective aggregator and focus instead on the sites that provide you with coupons that are useful and are likely to be accepted.

HACK #5:

Map Out Shopping Route

This trick is particularly useful in stores you visit often where you will be buying a variety of products. The best example would be your neighborhood supermarket.

Now you may think mapping the store is overdoing it, but it really pays to be methodical when shopping in large stores with tons of products. That's because it's far too easy to get distracted by other options that are either marked down or hard to find, leading you into a shopaholic frenzy. You'll tell yourself, "Oh, I've got to have this and this, and that too!" when in reality, YOU DON'T!

So, to cut down on impulse shopping—which only keeps you from being an effective shopper— map out the store using this approach:

1. When you arrive at the store, draw a rough map of all the sections you plan to visit on your trip. If you've decided to buy fruits, canned vegetables, cleaning products, and soap, your map should contain "produce (the fresh fruit and vegetable section)," "canned food section," "cleaning supplies," and "cosmetics."

2. Next, rank these sections with #1 produce, #2 canned food section, #3 cleaning supplies, and #4 cosmetics. This should correspond to the order that you will follow while you look for the actual products you want.

3. Finally, simply follow what's on your piece of paper (or you can opt to memorize it).

This way you avoid falling into the trap of becoming an impulsive shopper by buying something you didn't plan on buying. This strategy allows you to stick to your original plan and your budget. You will be amazed how much time and money you'll saving using this simple technique.

You'll also avoid the ultimate tragedy of a shopping trip gone awry—the all-dreaded buyer's remorse. Without planning ahead, you just might end up with items you'll regret buying once you get home. Sorry, no refunds.

When done properly, this method saves you time, money and space (because unwanted goods often end up in a pile garage).

ASSIGNMENT: With all that said, try this technique by setting up your own personal shopping map. By writing down a list of items you would like to buy, identifying the sections in the store, and mapping out your trip, you are taking the crucial steps necessary in planning a successful shopping trip.

HACK #6:

Prioritize with Shopping Pyramid

Most offline shoppers lack the ability to set priorities when it comes to shopping. When you think about all your wants and needs and the budget you must stick to make ends meet, it becomes clear just how important it is to make wise decisions with your money.

So, how do you go about prioritizing?

Creating a priority pyramid is an excellent way to distinguish the most important/expensive /desired items from the least wanted/expensive /desired items.

Follow these simple steps to create a priority pyramid before heading to the store:

1. Create a list of all the absolute necessities for your household's survival, most obviously food to eat. These items should be listed at the base of your pyramid.

2. Next add the most expensive/wanted/desired items just above the necessities listed at the bottom of the pyramid. Then work upward until you reach the top of the pyramid with the least expensive/wanted/desired items.

3. Use this list at the store, by purchasing the items at the bottom of the pyramid and working your way up.

This method helps you get a more satisfying shopping experience because it takes both your needs and your wants into account. For example, suppose your most expensive and desired item is a Tefal cooking pot. While at the store, you find that there's a great deal available for 3 pots for the price of 2. If this item is a priority on your pyramid, this might be the time to take advantage of the deal.

ASSIGNMENT: Try this out on your next shopping trip and see what a difference it can make. Remember to list your priorities with the most expensive/wanted/desired items at the base of the pyramid. Then, work upward, ending up with the cheapest, least wanted or desired items.

HACK #7:

The Envelope Technique

Effective shopping requires budgeting. While it's true that most of us work hard to keep money in our bank account, it can also be hard to resist the temptation of going on eBay or Amazon and a few clicks later, we've purchased things we really don't need.

One of the best solutions for this is using the "envelope method" of budgeting.

Here is how it's done:

1. After making a shopping list, divide it into groups. For example, when shopping at a grocery store your groups might look like this: fruits and veggies, cleaning products, cosmetics, meat, dairy, spices, starches, etc.

2. For each group set the amount you want to spend, for instance, $50 for fruits and vegetables, $70 for meats, $20 for dairy, etc.

3. Next, prepare an envelope for each group and fill them with cash in the amounts that you plan on spending. Make sure to label each envelope with the group and the amount budgeted.

4. Lastly, keep track of your budget by recording how much cash you put in the envelopes. This can be done digitally or manually on a piece of paper, whichever you prefer. Just don't skip this important step as it will help you budget more accurately when your needs change.

This method will give you peace of mind that you are spending within your means. By setting spending boundaries with the envelope method, you'll find that you will naturally pay close attention to deals and promotions, in order to stretch the value of each dollar.

<u>ASSIGNMENT</u>: Going forward, practice this envelope technique when you want to buy a considerable amount of groceries. It's also a great technique to use when shopping for clothing. This method allows you to get the things you want and need without spending an unreasonable amount of money.

HACK #8:

Operation Shopping Squad

Shopping is often a practice that is best done solo, as most of us want it done as quickly and effectively as possible. Bringing a shopping partner along has the potential to waste your valuable time or contribute to over-spending.

However, let's consider big shopping events like Black Friday or store clearance events. These events are crazy for many of us to handle alone. Everyone knows how these events can cause people to lose their minds.

To make them more manageable, consider assembling your own shopping squad.

That's right. Remember how there is safety in numbers? Well, you are going to need it to take on these shopping challenges of getting it first before sold out! Speed is everything with these door-buster events so you'll need to be prepared.

Here's how you go about setting up and utilizing your shopping commando:

1. Enlist people you know who can help you shop, like friends or family members. Think of people who are also planning on making similar purchases like appliances, clothing, etc.

2. As the sergeant of the shopping squad, you should set up the plan for your trip. This means creating a shopping priority pyramid and/or a shopping map, as previously described. Share them with the group as a suggestion for how to best tackle the big event.

3. Discuss your budget with the group, especially for people who are planning on buying the same items as

you. This way, everyone is prepared to snag up great deals the moment they come across them.

4. Once you've shared your map, priority list and budget, delegate the items. For instance, if you've picked your cousins Adam and Anna to shop with you for end-of-season clothing and fresh fruits and veggies, then you will assign each one of them a specific task— Anna gets the clothing while Adam takes care of the fruits and veggies.

5. Consider how to best communicate between one another during shopping. Your phones will do just fine to help everyone connect and share deals or discuss problems.

6. After getting all the items, each commando checks out (with or without the money you've provided). Then the group can meet outside the store. This is where all your preparations will come in handy. Inevitably, after the chaos of one of these events, there will be some

post-shopping organization necessary to sort everything out.

7. Finally, celebrate your shopping success with your friends and family and thank them for their help!

ASSIGNMENT: The next time you come across a big shopping event you are interested in, try recruiting a squad. You can even test this method by comparing your solo shopping trips with your commando shopping trips. Afterwards, ask yourself: How effective is the approach in terms of speed, ease of finding items, and respecting your list and budget?

HACK #9:

Target Specialty Stores

Shopping at warehouses like Costco or Sam's Club is a great way to save money, but don't miss out on smaller specialized stores either. These "hidden gems" are wonderful for those who want a different experience, whether that is trying out the latest fashions, eating eclectic foods or wanting healthier, local-sourced produce.

Stores to consider are pharmacies, sporting goods stores, bookstores, candle stores and other specialty stores.

If you want the quality of these stores without the high price tag, there are some simple strategies that can get you there.

Here's how to get the best deals at small retail shops:

- Ask if they have a loyalty card program, where you can accumulate points or get discount promotions.

- Visit the store at the end of each season, and you'll see items that were previously too expensive marked down by 15%, 20% or even 50%.

- Stay in touch with the stores on social media, especially if you want to get notified whenever there's a sale event or promotion going on.

ASSIGNMENT: As an assignment, think about what type of specialized goods you want to purchase, but often can get mislead with non-authentic cheaper version on eBay. For example, this could be "Seen On TV" workout equipments or aromatherapy oils. Find stores in your area that specialize in these products and investigate some of these ways to score some deals.

HACK #10:

Bulk Up at Warehouses

One of the absolute best ways to save money is by buying in bulk, rather than buying things one day at a time. This is why warehouse stores have exploded in popularity. If you aren't already buying non-perishables in bulk, chances are that you are paying too much.

To start saving money follow these steps:

1. Get a loyalty card or a member's card to get access to stores like Costco or Sam's Club. Or you can get a discount percentage as you pay for your merchandise at stores like Target. You'll also get access to information about new products, promotions, coupons, etc., sooner than other customers.

2. Look around these stores and see what will benefit you and what products are available in bulk. Here's a suggested list: milk, sugar, cereals, sodas, packaged meats, and canned vegetables and fruits. You may also want to stock other everyday items like cleaning products, toilet paper, and toothpaste. Check out prices on ordinary items like white t-shirts, thermos (for kids and adults) and underwear (not to be funny, but you'll save a lot by having these in quantities in your closet).

3. After you've made your choices, proceed to the cashier. If you are a member of the military, always ask for the military discount. These stores almost always grant this, so don't be afraid to ask and provide your military card.

Keep in mind, when planning a party (perhaps a birthday or holiday like Thanksgiving, 4th of July or Christmas), consider shopping at a warehouse store instead of your local grocery store. You'll be surprised how amazing their roasted turkeys can be, and you'll find it at a cheaper price too.

<u>ASSIGNMENT</u>: So this week, get a membership card from reputed warehouses near your area, and start shopping wisely to save money and time.

HACK #11:

Pierce into YOUR Shopping Crystal Ball

Now this hack is perfect if you're a parent shopping for children's clothing, though it can be useful in other areas as well.

The key is learning to predict the future. Now we don't mean that you need to be a modern day Nostradamus, but you do need to take a moment to ahead for what items you will be needing in the future.

The extra work in planning ahead will all be worth it once you've mastered this useful trick. Here are some tips to keep in mind:

- When it's the end of a season, look for items that are marked down now that you know you will need next year. For children's clothing, that means buying a size larger than they are now, to be used the following year. For example, for your 4-year-old you'd be looking for size 5 clothing. You'll find that these items will cost up to 50% or 60% less at the end of the season. So stock up on summer t-shirts in September or get a great deal on a winter jacket in April.

- Make sure you buy these end-of-season items in reasonable numbers. One strategy is to decrease the number as you pick items from head to toe. So, here the trick would be to, for example, pick 6 shirts (starting up), 3 jeans (going lower), 1 pair of shoes, etc. As you see, those are things people feel they need to renew every year, because they wear them every day. And, a pair of pants have less chance of getting dirty compared to T-shirts, so buying more discounted shirts than jeans make sense for proficient shoppers.

- Remember that you'll need to store these items as well, so you'll need space for that intended purpose. That means clearing your closet or making room in your attic. When it comes to clothing, consider storing them in bins or blanket bags (sold for $1 at the dollar store) labeled with the appropriate season. Or be more specific by labeling them "John's Winter Clothes for 2017," "Annabelle's Jacket for 2017," etc. This way it's obvious when they should be opened and for whom.

Using this strategy, you will save money and time, and you'll be prepared when the next winter season arrives.

ASSIGNMENT: So look for these marked down items from last season and start stocking them for the following year. Watch how you will save in terms of time, money and other resources for the year to come.

HACK 12:

Two Time's a Charm for Any Out-of-Season Items

Another way to maximize your shopping experience is to capitalize on things you know you will use every day. Whether it's clothing that's marked down or your favorite foods, why only take one item? Double your purchase instead.

So, this is what you should do:

- For items that are not likely to go out of style, like dark clothing (black, gray, or ocean blue) buy them in series of two once they are marked down. Also think about socks, underwear, t-shirts, dress shirts, etc.

- When it comes to non-perishables, you can double-up on the amount of items you usually buy like make 10 canned soups 20 or 6 boxes of hot cocoa 12 when they go on sale at the end of the season.

This way, you won't run out of the food you need, but you won't have items leftover 6 months from now either.

ASSIGNMENT: Practice this technique by considering what items you need that could be purchased in the off-season. Think about dark-colored clothing or non-perishable seasonal foodstuff. Try buying these items in a series of two.

HACK #13:

Luxury for Less

If you happen to have expensive tastes and crave luxury brands, there are still ways to save big on those items.

There are retailers which specialize in selling name-brand products such as Marc Jacobs, Chloe, Versace, Nike, Coach, and Adidas at substantial discounts. Many of these products are taken from stores like Nordstrom and sold at Marshalls, T.J. Maxx or Burlington Coat Factory.

Prices are amazingly low on some of the same products you can buy in the mall. In fact, take one look at the tag and you'll see the difference between the actual price of the item and the price charged by the store, which is often 50% lower. You might have to dig a bit to find what you need, but these stores are worth visiting.

Here are some useful guidelines for shopping in these discount stores:

- Look for products that you know are expensive, like perfumes/colognes, beauty products, and luxury beddings. For example, if you usually buy designer perfumes at Sephora, you'll be surprised to find these same perfumes for 30% to 50% cheaper in places like Marshalls.

- If available, get a membership card. This is an easy way to get an additional 15% to 30% off your purchases. These stores know that offering such deep discounts will ensure you'll be back for more great deals.

These are ideal stores for those who love quality items but either can't afford them or simply can't justify spending $200 on a bottle of perfume. Perhaps some people think that expensive perfume is a status symbol of some sort.

<u>ASSIGNMENT</u>: If you want to out-smart these overspending patrons, then shop at these stores and you'll smell like a million bucks without having to spend it!

HACK #14:

Shopping Locally at the Perishables' Source

As we pointed out earlier, shopping in-store for perishable food is the only way to ensure you are getting a quality product. To take that a step further, consider shopping at fresh produce markets, like farmers' markets, as opposed to grocery stores.

Shopping at these local markets gives you the opportunity to eat better for the following reasons:

- The products are grown using fewer pesticides than the food sold in supermarkets.

- The transportation of these products has less impact on the environment.

- It tastes better than other foodstuffs produced in large quantities.

- You get to buy a variety of goods, that are fresh from the farm or freshly baked including eggs, seasonal fruits and veggies, freshly baked cookies, flowers, etc.

To find out when and where these markets are, simply good old Google them. You can search your zip code for "fresh produce" or "farmers' markets," and you will find names and locations of local farmers' markets. Remember to note the times they are open as typically they only open once a week.

Prices at farmers' markets are surprisingly competitive too. While you really won't feel a big difference in the price, you sure will in the taste!

Because these events are only open at certain times, you'll want to stock up when you go. Here are some tips to take advantage of a trip to your local farmers' market:

- Look to buy a variety of fruits and veggies and other perishables like eggs.

- Talk to the sellers to gain information about their products so you know what you're buying.

- Try to negotiate when you can. Remember it's a market, not a store! So no price is set in stone. If you want to bulk up on large quantity of quality goods, by all means, ask for a discount.

- Ask how to best preserve their products so they will last longer. What can be frozen or canned? Baked goods can often be stored in a tin and your veggies will last longer in re-sealable bags. Don't hesitate to ask as they know they know their products best.

ASSIGNMENT: So, as an assignment, you will have to search "fresh produce markets" and familiarize yourself with the markets in your area. Plan to attend the next available market to see what it's all about.

HACK #15:

Stretching the Dollar for Brand Names

It's a blessing (and possibly a curse) to have so many options when it comes to shopping. The fact is, there's a market out there for every budget and every need.

For example, instead of buying your cleaning products from a grocery store, you can get cheaper versions at a dollar store. (Of course, there is no guarantee the quality will be the same.)

Here are several tips for making these high-quality products more affordable:

- During big shopping events, instead of focusing on big-ticket items, consider purchasing high-quality household items that you normally feel are too expensive. Think about cleaning products, cereals, soap, deodorants, etc. These products often are sold in bundles or packs with a 3 for $3 deal. Look for big brand names, like Tide, Ajax, etc.

- The advantage of big brand name products, they do create their own manufacturer coupons. So always keep the flyers or promotional mail that comes in the mail every day, and peruse them for coupons or deals.

- Consider sacrificing some of the gadgets you've been wanting and instead purchase the items you really need. For example, swap that expensive Japanese tea service you plan on buying on Black Friday for cleaning essentials, soaps, cereals, etc., that are also marked down during that period. In other words, re-work your shopping priorities by eliminating what you know you really don't need, and focus on the things you need that are now more affordable. (Recall our Priority Pyramid?) Prioritize for items such as flour, cake mixes, butter, or snacks for kids.

ASSIGNMENT: This technique helps you shop wisely by helping you focus on what you need. Now, to get some practice, here's an exercise for you:

1. Write down a list of items that you wish you could afford.

2. Narrow this list down, by eliminating less-useful items.

3. Replace these items with things you truly need like food and cleaning products.

INFO UNLOCKED:

Going Pro in Offline Shopping

To become a proficient shopper and ensure you are getting the best products at the best price, you need to leverage all the tricks of the trade.

As we mentioned, there are so many simple things you can do prior to going to the store: investigating the merchandise you are interested in, narrowing your choices, and gathering coupons.

Once at the store, there are even more ways to further ensure your shopping success. You've learned ways to work around the store and choose merchandise wisely while saving time and money. You know the value of shopping wisely and sticking to your priorities by getting what you truly need. You've also learned how to take advantage of big shopping events like Black Friday and after Christmas sales.

When purchasing groceries, use these hacks to get healthy, high-quality food for a fraction of the cost. There are so many ways to make products you never thought you could afford more attainable.

By learning to become a savvy shopper, you can save time and money while also finding the best products available. Start shopping offline like a pro today!